Contents

D1297867

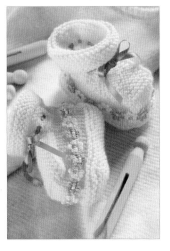

Daisy Chain

Materials:

1 x 50g ball cashmere baby fingering yarn
    in cream

20in of flower braiding

20in of deep pink baby ribbon

Needles:

1 pair size 5 knitting needles

Instructions:

Make two.

Using cream yarn, cast on 37 sts.

Row 1: knit.

Row 2: K1, *inc in next st, K15, inc in next st*,
K1, rep from * to * once, K1.

Row 3: knit.

Row 4: K2, *inc in next st, K15, inc in next st*,
K3, rep from * to * once, K2.

Row 5: knit.

Row 6: K3, * inc in next st, K15, inc in next st*,
K5, rep from * to * once, K3.

Row 7: knit.

Row 8: K4, *inc in next st, K15, inc in next st*,
K7, rep from * to * once, K4.

Row 9: knit.

Row 10: K5, *inc in next st, K15, inc in next st*,
K9, rep from * to * once, K5.

Row 11: knit.

Rows 12–29: beg with a knit row, cont in SS for
18 rows, ending with a purl row.

Row 30: K33, sl1, K1, psso, turn.

Row 31: sl1, K9, P2tog, turn.

Row 32: sl1, K9, sl1, K1, psso, turn.

Rows 33–48: rep rows 31 and 32 eight times.

Row 49: rep row 31.

Row 50: knit.

Rows 51–53: GS.

Make eyelet holes for the ribbon as follows:

Row 54: K1, *yo, K2tog*, rep from * to *
to end.

Row 55: knit.

Work a further 24 rows in GS. Bind off.

To make up the bootees

Work in all the yarn ends. Cut the braiding into
two equal lengths. Sew a piece of braid along
the center of the stockinette-stitch panel on the
side of each bootee. Sew up the foot and back
seam neatly. Turn over the garter-stitch
top to form a cuff. Cut the ribbon in half,
thread it through the holes at the ankle
(see Knitting Information on inside front
cover) and tie in a pretty bow.

Tiny Trainers

Materials:

1 x 50g ball DK baby yarn in denim blue

Oddment of DK baby yarn in bright red

Oddment of fingering yarn in dark blue
  for laces

Needles:

1 pair size 5 knitting needles

Instructions:

Make two.

Using denim blue yarn, cast on 27 sts.
Row 1: knit.
Row 2: K2, m1, K11, m1, K1, m1, K11, m1, K2
[31 sts].
Row 3: knit.
Row 4 : K2, m1, K12, m1, K3, m1, K12, m1, K2.
Row 5: knit.
Row 6: K2, m1, K13, m1, K5, m1, K13, m1, K2.
Row 7: knit.
Row 8: K2, m1, K14, m1, K7, m1, K14, m1, K2.
Row 9: knit.

To form the red edging around the base of
the bootee:
Rows 10–15: join in bright red yarn and work 6
rows in SS.
Break red and rejoin denim blue yarn.
Rows 16–25: work 10 rows in GS.
Rows 26–27: join in red yarn and work 2 rows in
GS.
Break red and cont in denim blue.
Shape instep as follows:
Row 28: K26, turn.
Row 29: K9, turn.
Row 30: K8, K2tog, turn.
Row 31: K8, K2togtbl, turn.
Rows 32–41: rep rows 30 and 31 five times, turn.
Row 42: K9, knit across rem sts on LH needle.
Row 43: knit across all sts.
Rows 44–61: work 18 rows in GS.
Break denim blue yarn and join in bright
red yarn.
Rows 62–65: work 4 rows in GS. Bind off.

To make up the bootees

Work in all the yarn ends. Working from the
wrong side, sew the red edging by catching
together, stitch by stitch, the 6 rows of SS at the
base of each bootee. This will form a neat ridge
on the right side of the work. Sew the seam on
the base of the foot and then join the leg seam,
matching the rows. Work lacing up the front of
the bootees using a large-eyed, blunt-ended
needle (see Knitting Information on inside front
cover), as you would on a real boot.

Simply Blue

Materials:

1 x 50g ball baby fingering yarn in blue

Needles:

1 pair size 5 knitting needles

Instructions:

Make two.
Cast on 37 sts.
Row 1: knit.
Row 2: K1, *inc in next st, K15, inc in next st, K1*, rep from * to *.
Row 3: knit.
Row 4: K2, *inc in next st, K15, inc in next st*, K3, rep from * to *, K2.
Row 5: knit.
Row 6: K3, *inc in next st, K15, inc in next st*, K5, rep from * to *, K3.
Row 7: knit.
Row 8: K4, *inc in next st, K15, inc in next st,* K7, rep from * to *, K4.
Row 9: knit.
Row 10: K5, *inc in next st, K15, inc in next st*, K9, rep from * to *, K5.
Row 11: knit.
Work ridge pattern as follows:
Row 12: knit.
Row 13: purl.
Row 14: knit.
Row 15: knit.
Row 16: purl.
Row 17: knit.

Rep rows 12–17 once.
Shape instep as follows:
Row 1: K33, sl1, K1, psso, turn.
Row 2: sl1, K9, P2tog, turn.
Row 3: sl1, K9, sl1, K1, psso, turn.
Rep rows 2 and 3 eight times.
Rep row 2.
Next row: knit.
Work 3 more rows in GS, decreasing 1 st in center of last row.
Work twisted rib as follows:
Next row: *K1tbl, P1*, rep from * to *.
Rep row 1 twenty times, bind off in rib.

To make up the bootees

Sew up the foot and back seams neatly. Turn over the ribbed top to form a cuff.

So Cute

Materials:

1 x 50g ball DK baby yarn in multi shade

40in of narrow baby ribbon in pink

Needles:

1 pair size 5 knitting needles

Instructions:

Make two.
Note: MB = make bobble (see Knitting Information on inside front cover).

Cast on 33 sts.
Row 1: knit.
Row 2: K2, m1, K14, m1, K1, m1, K14, m1, K2.
Row 3: knit.
Row 4: K2, m1, K16, m1, K1, m1, K16, m1, K2.
Row 5: knit.
Row 6: K2, m1, K18, m1, K1, m1, K18, m1, K2.
Row 7: knit.
Continue to inc in this way until 53 sts on needle.
Next row: purl.
Work a bobble row as follows:
(K4, MB) to last 3 sts, K3.
Next row: purl.
Work 2 rows in SS.
Shape instep as follows:
Next row: K24, K2tog, K1, K2togtbl, K24.
Next row: purl.
Next row: K23, K2tog, K1, K2togtbl, K23.
Next row: purl.
Continue to dec in this way until 37 sts rem, ending on a purl row.
Work 4 rows in SS.

Work a bobble row as follows:
K3, *MB, K4*, rep from * to * to last 4 sts, MB, K3.
Next row: purl.
Work 4 rows in GS, bind off.

To make up the bootees
Sew in the ends neatly. Sew up the foot and back seams. Cut the ribbon in half, then, using a large-eyed, blunt-ended needle, thread the ribbon through the knitting at the top of each bootee just below the bobble row. Tie the ribbon in a neat bow.

Pretty in Pink

Materials:

1 x 50g ball baby fingering yarn in bright pink

2 pink ribbon roses

Needles:

1 pair size 5 knitting needles

Instructions:

Right bootee

Cast on 48 sts.

Row 1: knit.

Row 2: (K2, m1, K1) twice, knit to last 6 sts, (K1, m1, K2) twice.

Row 3: knit.

Rows 4–5: rep rows 2 and 3 [56 sts].

Rows 6–7: knit.

Row 8: K25, (K1, m1) 6 times, knit to end [62 sts].

Rows 9–12: knit for 4 rows.

Rows 13–20: SS for 8 rows, beg with a knit row.

Shape foot as follows:

Row 21: K19, (K2tog) 12 times, knit to end [50 sts].

Row 22: P33, turn.

Row 23: (K2tog) 8 times, K1, turn.

Row 24: P10, turn.

Row 25: (K2tog) 5 times, K3, turn.

Bind off 11 sts, K to end. **

Work the ankle band as follows:

Next row: K13.

Next row: cast on 20 sts, knit to end.

Work the eyelet row as follows:

Knit to last 4 sts, yo, K2tog, K2.

Next 2 rows: knit.

Bind off.

Rejoin yarn to rem 13 sts and work 5 rows in GS, bind off.

Left bootee

Work as for right bootee to **.

Work the ankle band as follows:

Next row: K13.

Work 5 rows in GS, bind off.

Rejoin yarn to rem 13 sts, cast on 20 sts, knit to end.

Next row: knit.

Work the eyelet row as follows:

K2, K2tog, yo, knit to end.

Next 2 rows: knit.

Bind off.

To make up the bootees

Work in all the ends neatly. Using flat seams, join the underfoot, heel and back seams. Sew a ribbon rose to the front of each shoe (make sure they are very secure to eliminate any danger of the baby pulling them off). Make two twisted cords, each approximately 8–10in long (see Knitting Information on inside front cover). Take one cord and use a large-eyed, blunt-ended needle to thread it through a stitch on the ankle band, on the outer side of the shoe. To position the cord, fold the ankle band over the baby's foot and align it with the eyelet hole. Tie the cord in a small knot to secure, leaving two ends of equal length. Fold the ankle band over the front of the shoe and thread the cord through the eyelet hole. Tie it in a bow.

Baby Boy Stripes

Materials:

1 x 50g ball DK baby yarn in brown

Oddments of DK baby yarn in blue and green

Needles:

1 pair size 5 knitting needles

Instructions:

Make two.

Using brown yarn, cast on 27 sts.

Row 1: knit.

Row 2: K2, m1, K11, m1, K1, m1, K11, m1, K2 [31sts].

Row 3: knit.

Row 4: K2, m1, K12, m1, K3, m1, K12, m1, K2 [35 sts].

Row 5: knit.

Row 6: K2, m1, K13, m1, K5, m1, K13, m1, K2 [39 sts].

Row 7: knit.

Row 8: K2, m1, K14, m1, K7, m1, K14, m1, K2 [43 sts].

Row 9: knit.

Rows 10–15: join in blue yarn and work 6 rows in SS. (These rows, when stitched together on the wrong side of the work, form the small ridge around the bootee foot.)

Join in brown and green and work in GS.

Rows 16–17: knit in brown.

Rows 18–19: knit in green.

Rows 20–21: knit in blue.

Rows 22–27: rep rows 16–21.

Rows 28–29: knit in brown.

Continue in brown and shape instep as follows:

Row 30: K26, turn.

Row 31: K9, turn.

Row 32: K8, K2tog, turn.

Row 33: K8, K2togtbl, turn.

Rows 34–43: rep rows 32–33 five times, turn.

Row 44: K9, knit across rem sts on left-hand needle.

Row 45: knit across all sts.

Rows 46–47: GS.

Row 48: make eyelet holes. K2, *yo, K2tog, K1*, rep from * to * to last 2 sts, yo, K2tog.

Row 49: purl.

Work 20 rows in K1, P1 rib.

Break brown yarn and join in blue yarn.

Work 2 rows in K1, P1 rib.

Break blue yarn and join in green yarn.

Work 2 rows in K1, P1 rib, bind off in rib.

To make up the bootees

Work in all the ends neatly. Sew up the foot and back seam, matching the stripes as you do so. Turn down the ribbing to form the cuff on each bootee. Make two twisted cords approximately 8–10in long using two lengths of contrasting yarn (see Knitting Information on inside front cover). Thread through the holes at the ankle using a large-eyed, blunt-ended needle (again, see Knitting Information) and tie in a bow.

Bumble Bee Boots

Materials:

1 x 50g ball baby fingering yarn in black

1 x 50g ball baby fingering yarn in yellow

Oddment of baby fingering yarn in white

Needles:

1 pair size 5 knitting needles

Crochet hook

Instructions:

Make two.

Using black yarn, cast on 37 sts.

Rows 1–3: GS.

Join in yellow yarn and work the stripes in SS.

Rows 4–7: SS in yellow.

Rows 8–9: SS in black.

Rows 10–15: rep rows 4–9.

Rows 16–19: rep rows 4–7.

Break yellow.

Shape instep as follows:

Row 20: using black yarn, K24, turn.

Row 21: P11, turn.

Rows 22–25: join in yellow yarn and work 4 rows in SS.

Rows 26–27: join in black yarn and work 2 rows in SS.

Rows 28–31: join in yellow yarn and work 4 rows in SS.

Break yellow and continue in black only.

Rows 32–37: GS.

Break black.

Shape foot as follows:

With right-side facing, rejoin black yarn and pick up and knit 10 sts along first side of instep, 11 sts from instep, 10 sts along other side of instep, and knit across rem 13 sts [57 sts].

Work 15 rows in GS.

Next row: K1, *K2togtbl, K23, K2tog, K1*, rep from * to * to end of row.

Next row: knit.

Next row: K1, *K2togtbl, K21, K2tog, K1*, rep from * to * to end of row.

Next row: knit.

Next row: K1, *K2togtbl, K19, K2tog, K1*, rep from * to * to end of row.

Next row: knit.

Bind off.

To make up the bootees

Work in all the ends neatly. Join the foot and leg seams, matching the stripes as you do so. Using black yarn, make two pairs of antennae. For each pair, make a knitted cord by casting on 24 sts, then binding off. Work in the ends. Using a crochet hook, pull each end of one knitted cord through to the front of a bootee, positioning them as shown in the picture, and secure the cord in the center on the inside of the bootee. Curl each end of the antennae into a tiny ball and secure with a few stitches. Embroider the eyes and mouth using white and black yarn, using the picture for guidance.

Spring Flowers

Materials:

1 x 50g ball baby fingering yarn in white

Oddments of baby fingering yarn in lemon and green

40in narrow baby ribbon in white

Needles:

1 pair size 5 knitting needles

Instructions:

Make two.

Using white yarn, cast on 33 sts.

Rows 1–3: GS.

Work pattern as follows:

Row 4: (K3, P3) 5 times, K3.

Row 5: (P3, K3) 5 times, P3.

Rows 6–7: rep rows 4 and 5.

Row 8: (K3, P3) 5 times, K3.

Row 9: (P3, K3) 5 times, P3.

Rows 10–11: rep rows 8 and 9.

Rows 12–19: rep rows 4–11.

Row 20: K1, *yo, K2tog*, rep from * to * to end of row.

Row 21: purl.

Row 22: K23, turn.

Row 23: P13, turn and work on these sts for the instep.

Row 24: P2, K3, P3, K3, P2.

Row 25: K2, P3, K3, P3, K2.

Rows 26–27: rep rows 24–25.

Row 28: K2, P3, K3, P3, K2.

Row 29: P2, K3, P3, K3, P2.

Rows 30–31: rep rows 28 and 29.

Rows 32–35: work rows 4–7 again.

Break yarn and rejoin to inside edge of 10 sts. Pick up and knit these 10 sts, then pick up and knit 10 sts from first side of instep, 13 sts from instep, 10 sts along other side of instep, and finally knit across 10 sts on left-hand needle [53 sts].

Work 11 rows in GS.

Shape foot as follows:

Next row: *K1, K2tog, K21, K2tog*, rep from * to * once, K1.

Next row: K1, K2tog, knit to last 3 sts, K2tog, K1.

Next row: *K1, K2tog, K18, K2tog*, rep from * to * once, K1.

Next row: K1, K2tog, knit to last 3 sts, K2tog, K1.

Bind off.

To make up the bootees

Using the blunt-ended needle and lemon yarn, work tiny flowers using lazy daisy stitch randomly on the checkered top of the bootee. Using green yarn, embroider two tiny leaves beside each of the flowers. Work in the ends neatly. Join the foot and back seams. Thread ribbon through the eyelet holes at the ankles (see Knitting Information on inside front cover) and tie in a pretty bow.

Fairy Slippers

Materials:

1 x 50g ball cashmere baby fingering yarn
   in lilac

1 x 50g ball cashmere baby fingering yarn
   in yellow

Needles:

1 pair size 5 knitting needles

Instructions:

Make two.
Using lilac yarn, cast on 33 sts.
Row 1: knit.
Row 2: K2, m1, K14, m1, K1, m1, K14, m1, K2.
Row 3: knit.
Row 4: K2, m1, K16, m1, K1, m1, K16, m1, K2.
Row 5: knit.
Row 6: K2, m1, K18, m1, K1, m1, K18, m1, K2.
Row 7: knit.
Continue to inc in this way until 53 sts
on needle.
Join in yellow yarn.
Work 2 rows in SS.
Change to lilac yarn.
Next row: K24, K2tog, K1, sl1,
K1, psso, K24.
Next row: knit.
Change to yellow yarn.
Next row: K23, K2tog, K1, K2togtbl, K23.
Next row: purl.
Change to lilac yarn.
Next row: K22, K2tog, K1, K2togtbl, K22.
Next row: knit.
Change to yellow.

Next row: K21, K2tog, K1, K2togtbl, K21.
Next row: purl.
Continue decreasing in this way, working 1 st
less at both ends of each row and maintaining
striped pattern, until 37 sts remain.
Work 4 more rows in striped pattern.
Change to yellow yarn and make eyelet holes
as follows.
Next row: K1, *yo, K2tog*, rep from * to * to
end of row.
Next row: purl.
Break yellow and continue in lilac.
Work 8 rows in GS.
Bind off.

To make up the bootees

Work in all the ends neatly. Join the foot and
back seams, matching the stripes as you do so.
Make two twisted cords approximately 8–10in
long using yellow yarn (see Knitting Information
on inside front cover) and thread them through
the holes at the top of each bootee using a
large-eyed, blunt-ended needle (again, see
Knitting Information). Tie in a bow.

Roses and Violets

Materials:

1 x 50g ball baby fingering yarn in lilac
1 x 50g ball baby fingering yarn in pink
40in of matching pink baby ribbon

Needles:

1 pair size 5 knitting needles

Instructions:

Right bootee

Using lilac yarn, cast on 48 sts.
Row 1: knit.
Row 2: (K2, m1, K1) twice, knit to last 6 sts, (K1, m1, K2) twice.
Row 3: knit.
Rows 4–5: rep rows 2 and 3 [56 sts].
Rows 6–7: knit.
Row 8: K25, (K1, m1) 6 times, knit to end of row [62 sts].
Row 9: purl.
Join in pink and work in pattern as follows:
Row 10: K2 lilac, K1 pink, *K3 lilac, K1 pink*, rep from * to * to last 3 sts, K3 lilac.

Rows 11–13: SS in lilac.
Row 14: K4 lilac, *K1 pink, K3 lilac*, rep from * to * to last 2 sts, K2 lilac.
Rows 15–17: SS in lilac.
Row 18: rep row 10.
Rows 19–20: SS in lilac.
Break lilac.
Row 21: purl in pink.
Row 22: K19, (K2tog) 12 times, knit to end of row [50 sts].
Row 23: P33, turn.
Row 24: (K2tog) 8 times, K1, turn.
Row 25: P10, turn.
Row 26: (K2tog) 5 times, K3, turn.
Bind off 11 sts, knit to end. **
Work the ankle band as follows:
Next row: K13.
Next row: cast on 20 sts, knit to end.
Work the eyelet row as follows:
Knit to last 4 sts, yo, K2tog, K2.
Next 2 rows: knit.
Bind off.
Rejoin yarn to rem 13 sts and work 5 rows in GS.
Bind off.

Left bootee

Work as for right bootee to **.
Work the ankle band as follows:
Next row: K13.
Work 5 rows in GS.
Bind off.
Rejoin yarn to rem 13 sts, cast on 20 sts, knit to end.
Next row: knit.
Work the eyelet row as follows:
K2, K2tog, yo, knit to end.
Next 2 rows: knit.
Bind off.

Flowers

Make one pink and one lilac flower for each bootee.
Cast on 18 sts.
Row 1: knit.
Row 2: knit twice into each st across row.
Bind off.

To make up the bootees

Work in all the ends neatly. Using flat seams, join the underfoot, heel and back seams. Sew two flowers on to the front of each bootee (make sure they are very secure to eliminate any danger of the baby pulling them off). Cut the ribbon into two equal pieces. Take one ribbon and use a large-eyed, blunt-ended needle to thread it through a stitch on the ankle band, on the outer side of the shoe. To position the ribbon, fold the ankle band over the baby's foot and align it with the eyelet hole. Secure the ribbon with small stitches, leaving two ends of equal length. Fold the band over the front of the shoe and thread the ribbon through the eyelet hole. Tie in a bow.

Berry Bootees

Materials:

1 x 50g ball baby fingering yarn in green

1 x 50g ball baby fingering yarn in red

Oddments of baby fingering yarn in yellow
and white

Needles:

1 pair size 5 knitting needles

Instructions:

Make two.

Using green yarn, cast on 37 sts.

Rows 1–5: GS. Break green yarn.

Join in red.

Rows 6–9: SS.

Join in yellow.

Row 10: K4 red, K1 yellow, *K3 red, K1 yellow*,
rep from * to * to last 4 sts, K4 red.

Rows 11–15: using red, work 5 rows in SS, beg
with a purl row.

Row 16: K2 red, *K1 yellow, K3 red*, rep from *
to * to last 3 sts, K1 yellow, K2 red.

Rows 17–21: using red, work 5 rows in SS, beg
with a purl row.

Row 22: K4 red, K1 yellow, *K3 red, K1 yellow*,
rep from * to * to last 4 sts, K4 red.

Rows 23–25: using red, work 3 rows in SS, beg
with a purl row.

Join in green yarn.

Shape instep as follows:

Row 26: K13 green, K11 red.

Turn and work on these 11 sts for instep.

Row 27: purl in red.

Row 28: K3 red, K1 yellow, K3 red, K1 yellow,
K3 red.

Rows 29–33: using red, work 5 rows in SS, beg
with a purl row.

Row 34: K5 red, K1 yellow, K5 red.

Rows 35–39: using red, work 5 rows in SS, beg
with a purl row.

Row 40: K3 red, K1 yellow, K3 red, K1 yellow,
K3 red.

Row 41: purl in red.

Break red.

With right sides facing and using green yarn,
pick up and knit 10 sts along first side of instep,
11 sts from instep, 10 sts down other side of
instep, and knit across rem 13 sts [57 sts].

Work 15 rows in GS.

Shape foot as follows:

Next row: K1, * K2togtbl, K23, K2tog, K1*, rep
from * to * to end of row.

Next row: knit.

Next row: K1, * K2togtbl, K21, K2tog, K1*, rep
from * to * to end of row.

Next row: knit.

Next row: K1, *K2togtbl, K19, K2tog, K1*, rep
from * to * to end of row.

Next row: knit.

Bind off.

Strap

Make two.

Using green yarn, cast on 4 sts.

Work 36 rows in GS. Bind off.

Flowers

Make two.

Using white yarn, cast on 30 sts.

Row 1: K1, *bind off next 4 sts (1 st rem on needle), K1*, rep from * to * to end of row. Break yarn and run through sts on needle. Draw up tight to form flower shape and secure with a few sts. With yellow yarn, embroider a few French knots in center of flower.

To make up the bootees

Work in the ends neatly. Join the foot and back seams. Sew a flower to the center of each strap. Sew a strap across the ankle of each bootee, securing them firmly on each side.

Rosy Toes

Materials:

1 x 50g ball of DK baby yarn in white

Oddment of DK baby yarn in pale pink

2 pink ribbon rose motifs

40in narrow pink baby ribbon

Needles:

1 pair size 5 knitting needles

Instructions:

Make two.

Using white yarn, cast on 27 sts.
Row 1: knit.
Row 2: K2, m1, K11, m1, K1, m1, K11, m1, K2 [31 sts].
Row 3: knit.
Row 4: K2, m1, K12, m1, K3, m1, K12, m1, K2.
Row 5: knit.
Row 6: K2, m1, K13, m1, K5, m1, K13, m1, K2.
Row 7: knit.
Row 8: K2, m1, K14, m1, K7, m1, K14, m1, K2.
Row 9: knit.

Join in pink yarn and work picot border
as follows:
Rows 10–13: SS.
Row 14: K1, *yo, K2tog*, rep from * to * to end
of row.
Row 15: purl.
Rows 16–17: knit.
Break pink and rejoin white.
Rows 18–29: GS.
Shape instep as follows:
Row 30: K26, turn.
Row 31: K9, turn.
Row 32: K8, K2tog, turn.
Row 33: K8, K2togtbl, turn.
Rows 34–43: rep rows 32 and 33 five times, turn.
Row 44: K9, knit across rem sts on left-
hand needle.
Row 45: knit.
Work 18 rows in GS.
Break white and join in pink.
Work picot edging as follows:
Work 3 rows in SS.
Next row: K1, *yo, K2tog*, rep from * to * to
end of row.
Next row: purl.
Work 4 rows in SS. Bind off loosely.

To make up the bootees

Work in all the yarn ends. Working with the wrong sides facing, sew up the pink picot edging by matching the sides together stitch by stitch. This will form a neat picot edge on the right side of the work. Sew the seam on the base of each foot and then join the leg seams, matching the rows. Fold over the pink picot edging at the top of each bootee on to the wrong side of the work and catch it down all round the inside. Cut the ribbon into two equal lengths and thread a length through the holes at each ankle (see Knitting Information on inside front cover). Sew a ribbon rose motif firmly on to the toe of each bootee, so that the baby cannot pull them off.